Communion

Communion

Nancy Mackenzie

Ekstasis Editions

© Nancy Mackenzie 2010
Author photo: Phil Mackenzie

Published in 2010 by:
Ekstasis Editions Canada Ltd.   Ekstasis Editions
Box 8474, Main Postal Outlet   Box 571
Victoria BC V8W 3S1   Banff AB T1L 1E3

All rights reserved. No part of this book may be reproduced in any form without the written permission of the publisher, with the exception of brief passages in reviews. Any request for photocopying or other reproduction of any part of this book should be directed in writing to the publisher or to Access Copyright, One Yonge Street, Suite 800, Toronto, Ontario, Canada, M5E 1E5 Tel 416-868-1620, 1-800-893-5777, fax 416-868-1621, admin@accesscopyright.ca www.accesscopyright.ca

LIBRARY AND ARCHIVES CANADA CATALOGUING IN PUBLICATION

Mackenzie, Nancy
       Communion / Nancy Mackenzie.

Poems.
ISBN 978-1-897430-62-0

       I. Title.

PS8575.K4227C66 2010   C811'.54   C2010-906659-6

BRITISH COLUMBIA
ARTS COUNCIL
Supported by the Province of British Columbia

Communion has been published with the assistance of a grant from the British Columbia Arts Council administered by the Cultural Services Branch of British Columbia.

Printed and bound in Canada.

A soul that knows itself ... knows that its movement is not in a straight line ... but that it moves naturally in a circle around its inner centre [the One] ... and as the souls of the gods for ever move in expression of their divinity. To be a god is to be bound to that centre, while what stands apart from it is man the manifold and the beast.... In our present state, with part of us held down by the body, we are like a man whose feet stand in water while the rest of his body rises above the surface; and ascending in the self that is not immersed in body, we join the centre of ourselves to the centre of all things —and we are at rest.

Plotinus
The Enneads
VI.9.viii

Contents

Ancestors and Angels
    Telling the Truth   11
    Heredity and Intention   13
    Threshold   14
    Birth   16
    Family Angels   17
    Shipshape   19
    An Early Grace   20
    Rainstorm   22
    My Friend's Soothsayer has an Old Testament Experience   23
    Chess Pieces in the Park   24
    Exile   26
    Tabernacle   27
    Accord   28
    River Clams   29
    Spiritual Canticle   30

Fieldgrass Conversations
    Coming into Town   33
    Fruiting   34
    Ave Verum Corpus   35
    Collaboration   36
    Field Glasses   37
    Church Bells   38
    Oration on the Wisdom of Animals   39
    Sacrament   40
    Viaticum   42
    Knowing the Day   44
    Knowing the Night   45
    Mined Motifs   46
    Truce   48

Gate and Willow Fen
    Heartsease and Fennel   51
    Longing for the Greatest Thing   53
    Doctrine of Signatures   55
    Strawberry Creek   56
    At Laguna Beach   57

The River	58
River Fragment	60
Downed Deer	61
Ghost of a Chance	62
A Person is a Place	63
Witness to Age	64
Prayer for Wisdom	65
A Promise of Things to Come	67
Imago Mundi	68
Rain, Wiwaxy Peaks, Lake O'Hara	71
Request	73
Pining	75
Human Rune	76

Mediatrix

Umbilical	79
Autumn Crescendo	80
Three Crosses	82
Homemaking	83
Yamnuska	85
Nightingales and Time	86
Ovulation Symphony	87
Over the Moon	88
A Sentinel Among the Herds	89
Fruits and Offerings	90
Non-human Voices	91
Black and White	92
Strongroom	93
Christmas Baggage	94
Ivory Willow	96
Metaphorica	97
Curiosity Cabinet	99
Advice from Western Canadian Rockies	101
Schooling	102
Horse at Work	103
Horse under Saddle	104
Heart of Oak	106
A Woman is Strong	108
Suite #6	109
Notes and Acknowledgements	111

Ancestors and Angels

I have immortal longings in me
William Shakespeare

Telling the Truth

My father's letterhead was stamped with a horse
and his message was one of escape—
how he tried to find solace in his study
but the whole world pushed in from the garden.
Cloying funeral flowers the colour of blood
and shod mud tracks all around the door.

Miles away, at my door
I imagined a messenger on a winged horse
or angels, not thinking one of my blood
could devise such a means of escape.
He'd said ravens lined the barbed wire round his garden
and he kept the funeral procession from his study.

He sent cryptic crosswords from his study.
Deciphering these, I refused to answer my door
though now there were hoof beats in my garden.
I could not believe cancer left on a horse,
but then, maybe with myths I could escape
while some angel lined the lintel with blood.

And now genealogies and tracings of blood—
who gets cancer and who gets caught in the study?
I shouldn't try to escape—
if I wanted my father returning to my door
a figure out of myth, astride a horse
passaging through a garden.

What else explains my trampled garden?
The autumn turns leaves to blood.
If my mother is a raven, who sculpted the horse?
It hardly matters. Now the keys to father's study
hang by my back door
and there's no family left to escape.

When mom left I called horses to help her escape
from pain; they sprang forth in her garden.
She may have left the key in the door
but it's only because of our blood.
I saw it all around the candle in the study.
Burnt wax, the colophon of the horse.

Am I too late? What I remember is mother's horse
the abandoned swing in the garden. My father,
our blood, this pen and ink study; the art of escape.

Heredity and Intention

My ancestor calls, a quicksilver tempest, late
at night when I've already removed my jewels
their bright promise consigned to a box.

I clasp the phone in bare hands, listen
to the chthonic spirit returning moonlight
across the creek
casting a spell of the past.

Without my amulets and amber
I am powerless to ward off this omen
being only a woman
melting down to bone through phone.
By demeanour I condone this concocted elixir
become imbued with storied memories.

What am I but a drop of water on a high path
above a river, dripping down through Earth past rock
to a cavern where pictograms tell old stories
about a mare's early labour, a leggy newborn colt.

Aquifer, ancient water bubbling to surface
at Big Hill Springs. What am I but a pure spring
ancestral memory, spilling out on a sacred spot of prairie
the wild neigh of the herd
racing out of the mountain
through cord, to cradle.

Threshold

With anaesthesia the room's steel clinks
fall mute around you.

A small bone from the inner ear
spins in a silent arc, lodges in dust

puffs once by his sandaled foot.
You follow the angel to catch a glimpse
of something greater than yourself,
the guardian of what you are supposed to be.

He seems to be making an orderly tour
from a disused crypt
through stairs
to a netherworld.

You emerge through a columnar archway—
dovecote cooing and filtered sunlight. Koi
and courtyard flowers in a walled pond.

Across the courtyard
through a breezeway
a nurse in uniform
vanishes. Babies cry.

White robed, a strobe of passengers
follow the many-hued behemoth.
They too
angle for a glimpse,
into the mirror's antique frame.

Everyone exits to some secret plane.
Cicadas chorus again.
In the hallway, finally, your own reflection.

You approach this marvellous image.
At its surface another sun shines.
You exit into the courtyard's desert heat,
and anchored by the sun
lean your back to the well's lip.
Splashes of water, circles of fish, lilies.

The one you have been trailing comes,
washes the dust from your feet.
Dries each delicate toe with the hem of his cloak.

Over his shoulder you watch queues
of newly dead
file through   ziggurat   columns.

No-one joins your quiet hour.

He sits back on his hunkers, his wings
shielding you from the view.
Healed? you ask.
How did I come to be here?

When he speaks
you reach for your sandals, stand
kiss cheek-to-cheek.

Grasp this moment
every mirror
before you go.

Birth

She peers out through windows set in high stone walls
and sees wild clambering sweetpeas, dolphins leaping;
beyond which, the sea, its vastness a promise
like so much else the serious, oh-so-serious monks
withhold

while arguing about soul, baptism, arcane absolutes.

She questions their philosophy with *theosis*:
*If not now, then when? When will I be one nature
with God? If not here, then where? Must I be infant
in my potential all the days of my life?*

Her guardian, tethered as he is to her with haloed bonds
reaches for her with wings—oh he would tell her if he could
if she would listen, but she's impetuous, determined
to be born, to be free, to discover
to trick the wise ones, escape the womb.

*You ask what I see out the window? Why I would forsake
this sacred space? What else but the lure of beauty?*

*Ladies' bedstraw and clustered bellflower
along the boardwalk, through dunes
Scotland's cliffs
a waterfall's answer
pouring itself into the North Sea.*

Too late they rise en mass, too late. She's gone,
her guardian too, premature, perhaps, but more divine than human.
Guaranteed impetuosity all the days of her life
through her headlong rush to be born.

Family Angels

Colonialism has left a bad taste
in people's mouths
but my grandparents' angels
with strong, vast wing beats
traversed the Atlantic like so many
of their brethren
flocks, in fact, and independent
of Clifford Sifton's promises—those
broke the hearts of the immigrants—but
their angels knew what they were doing having scouted ahead
and soared with hope, optimism, grace
to a new undulating, prairie land.

My mother's angel a spirit formed of Earth
twigs, rocks, pebbles, branches, leaves, moss
a changeling energy devoid of wing
in its early years, nevertheless an angel
intent on guarding her hands, directing
them from cloth nappies and chalkboards
to pitchforks, dandy brush, oil paints, and clay
renderings of horses, the hands that also
twig and leaf and sinew
brushed bangs from my eyes.

My father's angel a spiral vortex of energy
spinning, ever weaving the primal energies
husbandry, business, commerce
always seeking animal-stamped coins
payment in full express. An angel seldom off in heaven
under judgement for his charge's folly
but always there, to save him from accidents.

My brother's angel—old, old, old with little or no
understanding of the child. Bigger
things in mind. Impatient, negligent even,
until the adult emerged, and now
rueful and forgiving, providing grandeur
through mountain top heli-skiing arcs
and intense days in glassed office towers.

My sister's angel a darker, fey sprite,
more masculine than feminine, more black loam
and grey sea than spring water and apple blossom.
More fruitful than flower. And zestful
invigorated, fecund, fertile, *duende* thin.

My angel, supplicant, wise, lets me stumble
and fall, follows me down creeks,
into farmer's fields. Finds me in the
heat of misunderstanding, guides me out
with a courtly offered hand, leads the dance
gracefully, elegantly, purpose is a
porpoise as bp Nichol said, and we, together
find ocean, beaches, wild, the wild.

Shipshape

*We are the mingled weave
that many hands have worked on*
    George Mackay Brown

My father's mother's nephew, Bob Andrews, with his sister Mary, looked after my dad when he had his seventh birthday in Scotland while Granny visited her mom after years of estrangement for having left the old country in the first place. "Cousin Bob" came over from Stirling in 1934, got a job working as a mason hauling hods and shaping mortar after a day of which he'd whistle on his way past Le Marchand Mansion determined to overtake Edmonton's fast-walking women.   He high-stepped it past the Celtic cross and St. Joseph's Basilica where stained glass distracted him from those ephemeral women with their husbands tucked at home and began to question his ability to decipher symbology relative to prophecy as if coming down the avenue with two stone blocks in his hand could improve the biblical messages writ there by artists who said what they had to say in pewter and coloured glass. He, being a British subject who calculated history out of the Great Pyramid's dimensions, noted the beauty of Moses whether or not an Edmonton sun shone through the church's upper reaches.

After the summer, Bob said farewell to Edmonton's prophets down at the Masonic Hall, and with calligraphy thanked my grandparents: Janet and George, 1924 Scottish immigrants married after Granddad's Sangudo experience with the misrepresenting remittance man and Janet's first year with the Métis overlooking the Saskatchewan River — its air today an historic ecosystem transpiring, shipshape over the mauve and persimmon city core.

Rain today mixes with diesel on Jasper Avenue's paved prairie cobblestones and the city's overwrought electrical lines—jewelled perches where sparrows and robins transmit news of rues and avenues. Familial air in my rain barrels and raindrop drumbeats like dancelings kicking their heels up below deck mid-ship across the Atlantic again sailing the spirits home.

An Early Grace

Edmonton is waiting
on the streets that run through my father's mind
his hand held gently in the jaws of a pup

that takes him to Wilson's Dairy
where Catholicism is, momentarily
not such a sin and he struggles
to recite the Beatitudes while Mr. Wilson
milks a cow and the city
grows up around Catlickers and Potlickers.

Edmonton is the train
pulling into Strathcona Station
where my cousin with a fluffy dog in her arms
drives a white Camaro full of friends, takes
me along for the ride to the farm
on 17th Street before Shell bought them out
and when the circular drive banked past full-time gardeners
and Saskatoon trees harboured mosquito hordes.

My grandmother, who once chased my father around her yard
on 108th and 68th with a wet facecloth
phones me. She's had the tea and Peak Freans out
they are now cold and put away. The robins
in her feeder bothered by blue jays
and when am I coming? The city
holds the bones of my ancestors
in Mount Pleasant Cemetery
where it's calm under the pines and firs
where my children shriek through paths of mud
and last fall my uncle's casket rested above ground
while we leafed cold-fingered through old albums:

my beautiful young mother a possibility
of love most lovely of young women
because this city, her brothers and sisters
raised her beyond their own mother's early death
and Granny at 100 welcomed an urn of her ash.

Touch this green leaf,
a needle through time
touches my father's gnarled hand.
The dog reaches for a stick in the undergrowth
the pair trot on past McKernan Lake, take
a trolley, hail Red McKenzie, boys again
on the Southside, dark falling, parents
settling down to an early grace.

Rainstorm

Who can bear the truth of all this surrender?
Who dares to abandon her power to banished prophecy?
Is it blasphemy to sit with a seer in the bookseller's cove?

By following rules of social engagement
while chitterbugs shared chalk-white teeth
over tea and scones at the public library
she drew close enough
to spread her shawl over lamplight.

Her face designed wispy curls,
she counted the stars in your head
doled them out like playing cards
cast your fortune and left
as if her talent ever meant more
than sidewalk chalk.

What did you expect? That
the ambiance of her jargon would clarify?
Her ambition is as pretty as yours:
temporary pictures of what-will-be.

Who voiced the cloud wisps out of the sky
and why were lies mixed with truth?
Is the struggle to express your raison d'être
worth it in the end? Pass the chalk
sweep the step dry, calm down.
Paint, sister. Foretell it again.

My Friend's Soothsayer has an Old Testament Experience

My friend's consulted with soothsayers before this
those who read rosemary entrails on deserted roads
birdsong in the ditches. Out here she speeds past
in her Audi, bound for a place to stop and think.

A blue angel on the roadside
stands lost on the highway with real news
about the Holy Spirit to deliver.
As the Audi passes, the angel fades
in slough muck under the willows
where a hedge witch finds her halo
pulls what she thinks is a velvet antler
finds what she thinks is an actress
blue with cold in her dripping wet white,
hauls her home to a mansion in the suburb.
Chintz and Persian carpet. Her guest
has a vision to share. The Holy Spirit experience
for a hedge witch? Well, she is my friend's soothsayer.

What was an angel doing on the roadside
after the reading? Searching for truth?
Did she mean to stop my friend as she drove off
to the nearest bar to write the ravings down?

Rosemary, a little bush of it
in the ditch. That's all the soothsayer wanted.
Instead this blessing from the wilderness
where only brick layers and salesmen
tread through disturbia
planning faux aquatic ecosystems
on the outskirts of town.

Chess Pieces in the Park
for Libby, 1979

I spy Libby working late
on nematodes in Patterson Hall
from my third-floor room in Horton House
with Nova Scotia weather
coming in from the Basin.

Ground level, in swirling snow
I shout up to the lab
pitch small stones against the glass.
Libby comes down, lets me in, agrees
to be persuaded out into the storm.

We walk in Wolfville through ice fog
in the snow with streetlights
showcasing the snowfall.
We reach Willowbank Cemetery
the quickest route to Libby's apartment
off Minas View Drive.

The snowfall
covers ancestors, not mine, those who
all those years ago, blessed me
with tonight's moment of communion
its ecru, aqua and cool grey
rubbed silver with stories,
the imagination's microscope.

We see ourselves astride words of a dove
puny among these monuments.

Granite saviours, crosses, lambs,
like God's chess pieces.
Even my solo return walk
whether predestined or a spurious moment
in my own game plan
leaves no more than footprints
in the snow.

Exile

Practice closing the curtain against the night
waif to the community's closed fist
at least its spokesperson does not hit you hidden
as you are behind your composure.

Face like a weak moon behind a dog's bark.
Another day, then, has ended
and your ancestors rest uneasily in their wonder
if under these stars this one will have the disposition
to fulfill the least of their dreams
one by one braided into the helix
while you count the carrots you dug up.

Scrub at the earth on the orange hide.
The moon another silent creature
behind autumn's scudding clouds, the dog
baying at the fence line. The Amur Cherry tree

staggering under this white weight.
The neighbourhood's resident trumpet boy
put to bed, the cat purrs loudly
on her sheepskin. Your children, arms
akimbo on their pallets and your man
in fits and starts before the muted baseball on tv.
How can silence ease the opening of that fist?

Your ancestors pull up their chairs to your hearth,
listen to your story. Under the earth
in the garden, hidden and childlike, the faces of bulbs
close their eyes to winter's sleep.

Tabernacle

I have another question—
but you can't expect to have all the answers
and still be whole, a living target
in a landscape of snow with sleet
slanting down, where

angel footprints in the manse
lead beyond the rim of candlelight.

I enter the Basilica, where heaven is a human creation
overhead in stained-glass parable, with saints.

In the pews, the noon-hour faithful drop
to knees like incense curls
ephemeral beings, where an angel's fire
consecrates the congregation
in the breath of the psalm.

And for that simple hour, the day's damp drear
disappears, a vapour of questions
that need not be asked. I have found
tongues of fire and speak not a word after communion

when angels descend from the Basilica's arched dome
come with us
as we filter through the bleak day.

Accord

Listen. You can almost hear the music
of the spheres. The people, crunching over snow
marvelling at ice sculptures, firepits, gathering
through the blizzard's aftermath aware of subtle chanting
from common trees like alder, willow, hawthorn,
these can yield such shelter, and memory or future.

It's the peace accord between the peoples
that yields today's celebration of winter
just as it held six thousand years ago. We hear
the words from a round moon-face arts organizer
imagine ourselves ages ago downriver
from Hawrelak Park's festival in Riverdale's floodplains.

Read these runes scratched upon our wrists
by chickadees, heed the drumming snowfeet
on the dwelling's rooftop, plunge our souls
into the moment, pour them round sun dogs in chill air.
The ghosts of the crushed bones gather and rise
spiral up through tepee smoke and quickened pulse.
Fill our nostrils with the smell of cooling gold.

Out in the white park above the North Saskatchewan River
frost maidens sweep the trails, cavort with wild abandon.
If you want something, you have to know how to give it.

River Clams

Tight lipped and unforgiving
the rancher's daughter fled her childhood
left behind games of spearing bedbugs with hatpins.

She stole a linen kerchief for her hair
and a horse to speed her

for the day. Rode hard
for the river encampment.
Traded a pound of folly
for a sack of clams,
sped back to the palisades
Fort Edmonton with its civilization.
Met up with the Factor
and the guide who would be her suitor.
Delighted him with her spirit.
Would a life with him
open trade, her silent secrets
river meltwater and steam
open, open?

Spiritual Canticle

I have not yet focused
on a background
of eternity. Is my canvas marred?

Come then on this inhale
lift my arm
see at its end
a paintbrush dipped in ochre
and on this exhale
begin a line.

No mapping. Just storytelling
and truth. The kind a water witch
finds with a willow wand.
The kind a mare knows
about her foal. The scent
as I/you/we breathe
is jasmine with a spindrift dew
ocean's edge now use lapis lazuli
pigments from Earth
to paint eternity always
one step ahead of me
the better distance
to dance at the easel.

Fieldgrass Conversations

How many times have I heard the locks close
And the larks take the keys
And hang them in heaven.

W.S. Merwin, *Migration*

Coming into Town

Communion, with Saskatoon blossoms,
on a country road's verge
with a city that rises and falls in the distance.

Edmonton on its map of river flowers,
amazingly green after the country's roadside hours
of snow, ice, snow, ice. A hockey town
planted in a wilderness of hardy bowers
offers glimpses of river's edge, the people's forge
a white chill of snow. We forgive the endless winter vista—
our city's recurrent theme. Come spring, the Saskatchewan tosses
and turns on her bed, never catching
fully, the sleep that history brings.
Time flows both ways here, the river
carries roe, minnows, grilse in her veins.

On shore, city councillors are in session again.
Edmonton's long summer night has kept them awake.

We walk into this day with birdsong in our veins
everyone's uneasy tornadoes spilling out of the sky.
Early morning mood builds fists to shake at the sun.
Vesper sparrows carry northern insects to young.
Love trysts in café courtyards
traffic sounds a mirage, the asphalt
sweats into another breathless night full of birdsong and promise;

the lure and call of the city's common wealth
on the riverbank with an artefact, the travel guide's
alphabetized entries for making sense
of our natures: Strathcona Arts Barns. The Legislature.
The Toonerville Trolley's century-old emotion-thought patterns
finding a home in Dad's mind. The wind whips
yesterday's newspaper in eddies of grit
the alley's idling taxi. On the street, mirrored,
glass-fronted buildings catch reflections.

Fruiting

When you no longer recognize your face, it's because an unknown ancestor has taken up residence for awhile.
        Henning Mankell

Intimations, how we remember those who have passed.
Flocks of geese, the gatherings of robins in the Ash
drunk on immanent euphoria and pre-migration.

This face I divulge in the lintel
a living stone, wind and time and circumstance
keep chiselling toward perfection.

My hands like Amur Maple bark
textured, delicately auburned, fingers offering perches
through the aerial repartee of boho robins.

That I am surrounded by oakwood
brings a smile for the little nameless flowers
rooted at my feet, my arms cradling their lush burgundy.

Intimations, apples,
the tree I have planted in view of my door.
Its beauty a presence reflected

when evening sun descends again, and again
searching indigo for the root of bliss. The wind's caress
etches another line and another.

My garden where the only sounds—beyond my sigh of bliss
an apple falling from the Thunderchild Crabapple
or the evening wren in the garden's Riverbank Grape.

Sunflower's face rustling on its tall stalk—
the chip and carve of a woodworker's inspired chiselling
in today's nocturne, chiming. *Come in.*

Ave Verum Corpus

This litany of my life
Great Plains childhood words
Strome Glen Farm—Lee's Hill
where Leslie's grey quarter horse stood
not hobbled, but out of choice
high on the knob, a grey silhouette
against distant mountains.

Lee, with her roan coat
own mind, stubborn will.
Wise sister-mare knew more
always
than I did
about how the herd runs
but not through pastured dreams

kept rural and local by so many
section lines
well-sites
badger holes
the old rocks lichened
Indian tomahawk heads
white-tail and the black
coyote.

These are songs of my sleep
great horned owl
binder twine about my feet.

Collaboration

I listen to the voices of trees
in early spring
song of mist thickening over melting snow
song of wind in robin's wing
song of sunlight dappling forest floors.

Patches of thick bracken like living wicker
pillow my old woolen coat.
I call down the phantom of the North
and she settles in her perch across the valley
in song of gyrfalcon landing on birch.

Behind me
white-tailed deer graze and flick
up along south-faced hills
where kinnikinnick
grows in winged horse shapes
song of moccasined feet
jeaned calves brushing berry blossoms.

I hear valley whispers
on warm breaths of wind
psalm of prairie bud yearning for sun.
I call down the hawk screech
song of horse skin thermals bolting
and cold front cadences clipping over the valley's canopy
song of birds of prey and antlered beasts
sheltered for the day.

My voice a back-forty descant solar oratorio
song of woman walking away.

Iced-up ponds hold footprints:
I have left my own
at the barbed-wire crossing,
and I have called the dogs.

Field Glasses

But I never question these synaptic flits
between bulrush and printed page.
Below my window acreage undulates.
A sand hill crane wades through heat on stilts
and grasshoppers sing prairie wool songs.
Acrobatic wordsmiths grown as fat
and powerful as summer
propped on my knees.

The house in a coulee.
Mint-tongued wind riffles page's flat words
its taste for font ascenders disappears.
An aft wind shifts field ladders
for the hopper's high wire act.
Grasshopper typescript perches and flings
from bending waves of timothy.
In voracious mouths, grasshoppers carry letters
in double wings, morphing *corpus pontiflex*.

Plotlines scroll across the bloom.

My eyes on the question mark
beheaded grasses bend
and lift, ragged attempts
to underscore what is left
with a borrowed eloquence.

Church Bells

May I kiss this ring, this ring
with a world of truth in it? Hear
the humming silence of a God
who listens to my prayers, suspends
my weight from the bell tower

and lifts the ladder out from
under me? A kiss that centres
on a gemstone of the earth where
water at Bridal Falls mists
on granite faces
where cedar breath rises. Gravity

is a steady thing at the coast.
Solid as air and tidal pools.
O let me buss the clouds
with the ebullience
of this kiss, and speak

so that what resounds
is an echo of each pure note.

Oration on the Wisdom of Animals

Now he taps me lightly on the calf, each step
a display of courage and invitation
like a conversation about illness or divorce.

Such are the battles we fight
up and down the ladders of our hearts.

Having won the skirmish
for a gnarly staff-sized stick
Laddie trots at my heels
taps me lightly on the calf, each step
a display of courage and invitation.

Question, question. When the challenge
on the narrow trail up from the water's edge
comes bounding toward you, teeth bared
do you drop your conviction
and wrestle the danger
or hold on tight and growl?

Sacrament

Rivers pool and whirl
steady as she goes   the world ripples.

I leave the world's eddies   climb onto the jutting rock overhang.
Below, in the deep, water flows
in communion, clover-boxed.
After church, high on truffles and cake
ate it and was still green water
after Mass with the North Saskatchewan River
or Jumping Pound, or Big Hill Springs
pools, memories, and power working within.

Or being in the alpine, alone at the altar,
breathing bracing air, on fallen knees,
wisps of hair frame my face
time-lapsed photography scrolling to a beadstop
on my rosary; a crow flaps down an aisle of trees before me
night-drop; where to nestle for night in a barren birch.

Throaty hymns and arias around as we
hold hands in pews, recite *Our Father*
count on one another: one for the wafer
another for the clock, one for the wine
another for the cloth.

Church-poised-mind with all the fallen notes
of hands, prayers, words, ghosts, wonder.

Wonder and the even breath of this: flocks of autumn robins
roosting in Mountain Ash between the church
and the hall where the Women's League
serves tea and truffles, the snow clouds
angels outside as we traipse across early snow

the omnipresent "we" in a wafer
in a still, green pool
ripples two thousand years
in a moment
in a moment
in a moment
of bliss—

Viaticum
– the passing over to eternal life
for David

Spring melt on the boulevard
between Highway 2 north and south
yields a proud concoction of lab and collie
tail wagging, stick-carrying, trotting.

We're heading north, home from the last weekend skiing.
At 120 kilometres per hour I glimpse the dog
and wonder how he'll cross one side of the road
or the other and I'm touched by
glimmers of old spirits this weekend,
medicine of immortality,
when skiing at Sunshine.

In blue sky schussed by brief blizzards
an intimate presence took shape
as my daughter clamped boots into bindings behind me
and I reached for skis propped on the lodge deck.

Alpine sun and stillness flashed around us
with grey snow masks on Goat's Eye.
Days after his death, David may not yet have left Earth.
Some part of his song, wind along the aspens
a memory fluted through

David with his old leather jacket
the organizer's voice at Stroll of Poets
board meetings
the successful advocate at readings.
David and his apologetic smile,
handing readers the board's white envelope of cash.

This afternoon, angling home, another reward:
I saw an eagle on the snow
beside an open gift of water;
a raven's shadow on the ice;
and a spirit or a memory—
neither one
nor the other; we were heading north
from the last weekend skiing.

Knowing the Day

Sunday afternoon and the bulrushes
speak their hoarse homilies
pledge their sweet release.

As if a schematic of the ecosystem's logic
could speak through the door of its voice
sing of the brine shrimp two-step, the frog honky tonk
could turn into something like reeds for the tuning
a black bag full of air and the swollen gift of lungs.

A blackbird descends to a reedy perch
trills its questions in the slough's ether
takes wing, its talon ripping the rush flesh
and myriad punctuating seedpods drum
lilting drunkenly on blackwood air.

Knowing the Night

I am sleeping on a bed of reeds
that catch my breath and make music
carried into sky's long ache
with poplar snow clinging
to nearby
tree branches
awaiting my movement

the trail of my fingertips

over the supple bark,
my song
to release the dance of the lazy afternoon.

Yearning between days.
Descending dreams the celestial music weaves.

At the river's gate:
the cough of the watchman
the flick of a coyote's tail
leads me in my nightgown
from one stone to the next, a dust mote or a breath
in search of the alert genius, aware of the changes
I have become.

Mined Motifs

Stretch flat the tanned hide again
script the dreamsong with prairie pigments.
One hears the echoed drumbeat
from the frog pond, a blindness
built from an excess of booktalk. Take

down this message then
as you gather the thought threads:
wolf mange, brown bear, black spider.

Wolf Rune
Willow gray revenant
road-denned, embarks
on the narrow cart path
depressed but fiercely able
to defend.

Bear Rune
Stands tall, roars an embrace.

Black Spider Rune
O so lace woven, filigreed.
This innumerable guest nesting
in my ear. The brood
slips out at Astrid's place
with the song of the salmon-seer.
But woven into the drum skin
in inky calligraphy? I think not.
Snowfall on the distant road
another ink blot.

Half-curtain
Window glimpsed daysnow opens the view.
Could this be the opening
I'm meant to seek? If so, the skin twitch
neath my pjs assuaged, fomented.
Careful, careful, the spring hides winter
up her sleeve.

Daystar
Age, that glowing angel, does her windowsill tiptoe.
Her knowing smile eases the mind. We agree on this:
today's openness, a thin veil time-frayed
with river-blue embroidery flowy along the edges.

Truce

From the paddock by the road
with the pine scent and owl's perch
we might gather what we need from the ground,
saddle Thoroughbreds,
ride out the back gate.

Under the cello's muse, stars.
Our soft croon breathes through night air
canter, trot, walk.   Transitions *sans* thought.
When we dream   a little creek silvers
near our campfire
and the gods might step
from the feathers that we took.

Gate and Willow Fen

At dusk I turned for home
and I saw my waving child,
A dancer in the blue hour,
And I grew wild.

Kevin Crossley-Holland

Heartsease and Fennel

There is a legend about a doorway through Earth
where healing begins. Fictions born through memory,
housed next the herb beds, the green Godhead.
Pan piping in the reeds along the river's kiss.
Sit here awhile at my hearth; let us break bread
trace the roots of colonial scandal.

How our unknown ancestors tried to reconcile scandal
leaving one land to oust others from choice Earth
power rising along the neat rows of wheat; baked bread.
Greed shrithing along limn lines and undulating memory.
The sea voyage, the rapture began with a kiss
and never ended, the fields a golden Godhead.

Dream if you must, but eventually your Godhead
wakes and delivers the report of personal scandal.
You think you can blame it on the angel's kiss
but evidence of your folly, your greed upon Earth
comes down from the highest place into memory
the storehouse at which hearth we take bread.

We take and eat this bread
thinking to reproduce Godhead
the core of our memory
a scattered, secret, forbidden rapture; a scandal
lamented in Heaven as it is on Earth.
Where is Justice with her fiery kiss?

The soul, enchanted by humanity, returns Earth's kiss
and reaps, oh how she reaps peace, the bread
of life. For all our longing to master Earth
we disparage the immateriality of Godhead
resurface herb beds and heartlands; think it not a scandal.
We may be co-creators but we have selective memory.

Agriculture. It's the taming, toiling midsummer memory.
Angels, sowers, reapers waking one another with a kiss
springtime theology as extinct as scandal—
what is left on the threshing floor when the oven births bread.
There is no dignity in a refutation of Godhead
and yet, and yet we claim to love Earth.

Let's be clear about Godhead and the angel's kiss.
We are sustained by deep dungeons for memory.
Here upon Earth's hearth our expectations a scandal.

Longing for the Greatest Thing

Illumination is the satisfying of desire to those who long for the greatest thing.
>   Gregory of Nazianzus

Who would shine light
on this cage?
There is thunder
and underfoot: an abyss
the tar sands.

Our planetary migrations
both cause and consequence
of global warming.

Jump, and the old ones
are waiting
with their incomprehensible faces
their hands working with stones and bitumen.

What religion has ever responded
to the planet's desecration
with more than wailing? We see ourselves
as divine blessings wherever we go.

Of course darkness also affects the blind.
Their oracular divinations suggest
possibilities of rebirth
even out of the secrets of tar sands
passed from generation to generation
by toolmakers long ago.

Never mind our predatory natures
we brought horses and goods to trade.
What happened to advice from the wise to the wise?
On the surface, holocausts, a grace lost
in an exuberance of ears plugged
with the certainty of divine right.

Are we God's instruments
and what is the greatest thing?

Flintknappers working with obsidian
on the riverbank
20,000 years ago left a poetry
sometimes more visible and incarnate
between today's tongue and ear
than stories about the Creator or birch canoes.

The land carries its secrets about all these times
these peoples, their songs, stories, legends
but *angels do not need to pass through the door of the tongue
to have speech with one another, or with us.*

Doctrine of Signatures

The river's signature
reveals a flawless interlocutor
capable of powering factories
windmills tilting along Alberta's plains.

But no
we see instead the forgery
of run-off
unwanted oil slicks in city limits
bitumen by-products downstream
and sulphur pellets dusting the rail yards.

Whatever potencies the river
flailing about mutely
with her inky hands
has striven to record for our illiteracy
have been lost, an "x" on a treaty.

Faceless, mute, and unrelenting
in her tendency to besmirch usurpers

she will continue writing her name
on the hill brow, the tumbled stones
the vast esses meandering down from the mountains.

Strawberry Creek

What would you have me answer
that I do not know your name?
What else did the willow tell you
she, young and pliant, assured me a hello
welcoming me to your deathplace
like one who belongs. A ghost
at my window, the coyote's song at the sill
these are things I can attest to
even as I farm words from the plantings
of long ago.

At Laguna Beach

Catie
there are flowers along
Pacific Coast Highway
for which you have no name.

Like a memory
one friend holds dear
and the other has forgotten.

Like a part human
part infinite love
the surf returns
to the shore.   *Oleander*
you text
the single word
a found shell on the beach.

Put it to my ear
remember at last
why the journey
holds echoes
part eternal part pure now.

The River

So the gift of an image is that it affords
a place to watch your soul,
precisely what it is doing.
            James Hillman

What slips beneath the surface
interstitial, end of days.

Deliberate elk emerges, a mythical being
on the far shore. The river
pools downstream, above which
a young girl
holding a fishing rod
lolls back against dark green grass
on the sloped bank, asleep.

Water shadows flicker.
The elk, forest-bound
where elm and spruce wave warnings.

The girl-trout trudging back to town
with her Maxwell House coffee can
and a mutant fish gasping
in the river's breath.

The river watches
with clouds fast on her face.

It's such a small tract of river
wending through a city
population one million. Has
anyone counted thresholds
for population growth
against the sun's fierce effort
to see itself reflected

in the Saskatchewan Glacier's face
or is it all moon shadow
and phases, the kind of tick talk
that keeps people coming
oblivious to the source
or destination of this quiet river
that even now, even now
only hums under her breath,
content.

River Fragment

Magazine wisdom offers modus operandi
office parties, family tensions, love escapades

and I try out the mindset for a day or two
its sturgeon slowness settles deep.

Psyche eventually rejects the modern, calmly
covers the column advice with river silt.

Currents roll over the now, churn up prehistorica
memorabilia, a fish's jaw, a spine. Instinct

shudders with repressed wisdom
or old body over mind.

Downed Deer

Antlers broken in a chain-link fence
jaw slack from terror and pain
a four-point stag found refuge
in a willow grove
among paintbrush and wild wheat
within earshot of the Saskatchewan.

Sometimes we stumble alone there
or in pairs commiserating about betrayal
the loopholes and traps used by those we trusted
to hold us prisoner to their power.
Cast aside and derided for our all-too-human beauty
we seek sanctuary in nature
where, cowering, we may discover mercy.

Ghost of a Chance

For the love of our ghosts
we wait for history, its "one damn thing after another."
We are all survivors on stolen habitat.

Where work trucks line up like caskets in open air
all this urban space, spoils of war.
Where is our tribute, our reverence
for those quiet rays in the morning mist?

Has it faded like ghosts in daylight
invisible, yet present
like Earth's current call to arms?

A Person is a Place

If the eyes could see through a glass darkly
to Strome Glen Farm, a small acreage now bulldozed
under residential roads with the prairie skirting
a rose-lined road in the east
several paddocks, a horse barn, and shelters.

As if "home" could mean something beyond
a kitchen door, a dog in the yard, and
a need to find the spice cupboard
every place I go. Sage dust and rosemary's
clean needles and oregano, basil, thyme,
poignant with their earthliness.
The welcoming warmth of oven roast.
As if the nose
could find with the rattle of the drawer
or clattersound at the counter
grasping the garlic press, releasing
the beginnings of Caesar salad
or mushrooms
garlic and butter. The right mixture to open
that forever closed kitchen door on the old farm.
A scent of wolf willow blossom
and sage as cattle wrap tongues
around last year's prairie wool
yank and chew, tromp through
the field gate and graze.

The house grows older when I hear
voices of parents, owl in the trees,
dog in my arms, leap
up the stairs still a daughter
to see light fading
on couches, cobwebs, echoes.

Witness to Age

Do you remember that spring night
in 2003 when you were ten
and I forty-four? How the snow-wind
whistled through a crack in the front door's seal?
You smiled with the tips of your lower canines
barely etched on your gums
and lay backwards on your bed
upon your elbow, one knee crooked
opposite foot pushed under your pillow.
Tigger purred from her spot
in the rumpled covers along the wall
and I stood, pajamas strung over my shoulder
on my way to the bath.
"Mom," you said, "Who's going to
look after me
when I'm old?"
I held my pajamas over my face and wept
for I could not answer, "I will."
Do you remember my answer?
And look for me
when the snow-wind
buffets your door.

Prayer for Wisdom

It's like that stunning moment of paradigm shift
when everything hectic
panic stress movement deadlines
everything people traffic the club
music sports cooking action reading
talking parenting befriending confiding

rushing stops

all of it collides in this moment
and in an instance of clarity you see
how to pray for wisdom.

You stand on a hilltop
with the view of your life
completely in perspective.

You wait for the moment you've been waiting for
when you alone are recipient and
all the colors collide into you.

The snow melts in the rain
wing beat wet black
wool to dry down the animal skin

timepiece lost in the high grasses
azimuth facing north
lost destination

lost in the round around
circling road round the mountainside
the lake steep and far below

flight over the wet pavement
or snow too, find a grizzly bear
walking down the forest.

Somewhere the universe continues its celestial
orchestration and you, part peace, part harmony
gradually hike down from your hilltop

a mere mortal in the gather dusk.

A Promise of Things to Come

Advent used to be holy
but we fail to find it anywhere
in cardboard creations and cartoon figures
strung out along Candy Cane Lane.

Further out, past the suburbs
along curved and elegant iters
with Saskatoons cut back for berm
seasonal charms gaudify roadside shops.

Even boutiques with their swish renditions
offer too much, leave too little
to our gathering for the promise.
Have you heard—on a cold vast night

when you take the garbage
out through the thin air to the back gate
and look, at those amazing stars
a certain echo, your breath, perhaps

infusing your heart with a current of sound
a drum, and a welcoming carol?

Imago Mundi

1.

An immature eagle hunts from South Beach to First Point
where the sea calls and the wind answers
as I scour the beach for jellyfish
sea stars
and geoduck shells.

Under a shell
of understanding: scuttling beach crabs.

Wind careens around Mace's Point
under a broad-winged black eagle
lifts spindrift, currents, and tides.

Near First Point the shoreline at low tide
reveals, abandoned between two rocks,
a harbour seal pup.

Slow wind, a seagull hovers over my head
with its vertical lift
its workmanlike clam-drop
and fall to the opened treat splashed out on sand.

The waves break far out over the bouldered beach
while the sou'easter flings spindrift
while the waves break over the moorings
while the wind
rips through the channel
between our island and the mainland
and the harbour seal pup
anchored between two rocks
waits for the tide to change.

Beachcombing, I find its eyes
break me
and a greater spirit
mallet and chisel
pounds into my joints
and every opening.

Spindrift, wisps of the sea on salt wind.
Listen, a shell sound, the world
refurbished up-island by hammer-blow and wood saw.

These echoes of today like a bell tolling
quicken my desire for perfectly knowing what to do
with what I've found.

2.

Inside the cottage-by-the-sea
steam rises from my broken teacup
and out back my husband chops kindling
for the stove. Later, I will haul water
clean crab, peel prawns
loiter under the day star, echoes
of today like a bell tolling
quicken my desire
though not for the bone-breaking
mallet and chisel: I am a shell.

I break like water on stone
and a spirit inundates
every opening.

At First Point the tide rises
after a day of drying winds.
The seal pup is not the next day's dead thing
rolling at the shore's lip
under the government wharf
but swims out, we hope
across the sea to the Copeland Islands
beyond the moorings, otters toying with coiled ropes by the boats,
soft eyed through the weight of water
with its mother.

Rain, Wiwaxy Peaks, Lake O'Hara
oil on cardboard
1924 or 1925
J.E.H. MacDonald

Snow early turning to rain.
Wood wet for fire

MacDonald's extra paint daubs over-painted with grey = raindrops
as if trying to hide something, the view, studio finish
doctrine, or the Wiwaxy peak along the cardboard edge.
Palette spiral twists and flows, the pinnacle omnipresent
with its involuntarily curious shape
pelting wind strokes in my mind.

Named in 1894 by Samuel Allen
of the Lake Louise Club, Wiwaxy, Wiwaxy
for windy, a Nakoda word,
while the wind in the tamarack boughs
made harmony with the music of the waterfall
and he camped by what he called Gorge of the Winds.

MacDonald, sometime later, 1924 or 1925,
with his CPR passes to the Rockies
returning, like the wind, to create en plein air
for you and me, this windy world, this rain, this lake
the lake, the lake, its echo in his mind
calling him back for another glimpse
of its *emerald and violet...*
emerald and malachite,
and jade,
and rainbow green.

In my mind, green, the beginning again, of the world
created upthrusts, pinnacles, painted squares
of image-after-image,
a place of healing, wholeness,
the balance of the universe in rain,
in mountain, in *spiritus sanctus*
where presence of the Nakoda Wakonda, Wakonda, the Great Spirit
breathes life into the fire   by the lake
in the mountains, en plein air.

Request

I want to see God
in a glacier
in the river that carries its grace
to the sea.

I want to measure myself
against the experience
of ice and mountains.
See my face in campfire flames.

Will you trust me
to tell you what I find? Promises
are small white mouse bones
in owl pellets.

I want to find the lodges
where mountain folk
rest their heads,
heed the Nakoda wind in alpine larches
shiver with my husband beside me.

Shelter
with a bottle of wine
saved for the occasion.
An owl, a guitar,
and the bluegrass boys
smiling their welcome
after all those years of darkness
standing
between the river's shores.

I want beauty
even on cold, grey days.
Soup for lunch
and dry socks.

Later, I'll look for white feathers
on the Earth's snag.
Begin to share the blessings
from inside a coyote's yelp.
The marrow from my bones
ciphering the rivulet dialect
and the salmonid song
as the season turns again
with the glacier's slow tilt
and the slow, slow
quick, quick
of the water, dance: Saskatchewan Glacier.

Columbia Icefields.

Over which, if you cannot send me
let the little bones erode
and the owl hunt for more.

Pining

I want a map with clear directions
cinnamon rivers, hot codas, divine crescendos
windward, directions to sacred high ground.

I want lilac fresh from the garden
full lungs, a sunset-blessed heart
a pine forest and weathered standing stones.

I want demarcated distances. A trustworthy scale
B flat or F sharp major. I want traffic swishing down the freeway
easy access, healed wounds, a late fall light, and a hearth.

Tinntabulations, dove song in the morning
allegros, smoky coffee smell, pancakes and sausages on the porch wind
a window, a window streaked with gray-and-pink-rhythm.

Day after day, in strong arms, a harp suspended above the water
so the zephyrs may trail their bloodsongs
into the crystal cirque
and when evening with its soft skin
turns on a bed of desert sand
a brouhaha, a benevolence,
and a glass of the finest, purest river
with you.

Human Rune

I am dissatisfied
with the land's lie. I choose to change the horizon
dissolve corridors between bone mother's bedrock

trust in architects of today's new theorems

who build lily-shaped towers, moss-strewn trails
through city parks and cultivate gardens near schoolyards
where we teach our offspring to count and read
always with the decade's new insight into what was once thought old.

We teach one another about grief
and all the bondages of obedience
with two faces of the colonist: fear and pleasure.

Find a palm-sized stone
smooth and voiced-over
with its water knowledge
here will I inscribe my human rune
toss it
into places where ghosts wail
and monks "ohm." The
air. Suspension. And prototype.
I am always the inventor
tool making and writing on walls.

Mediatrix

So long as you have the opportunity,
get down to work and do your duty.

Hildegard of Bingen to the abbess at Elostat

Umbilical

After pregnancy I said I would never again be so connected
to another life. I was wrong. There is a before and an after.

Mapping geodetic lines through poplar, willow leaf and prairie wool;
where bulrushes part, a muskrat slides into the water.
Mint on airwaves, transboundary, one frontier to another.
A horse gallops up a roan hill in the heat dodging gopher holes.
A dog's lithe alertness, and me, pressed into this tawny hill.

Wordsmithing for clients, grasping for meaning in magpie flight.
Saddle, horse in from the paddock, forge stench at the cross-ties.
New ink, a calligraphy pen, fingertip control through reins.
Country lanes after dressage, each day widening the gap
between mother and child; the immanent moans like a dove.

Autumn Crescendo

Their hollow bones flutes
their lithe bodies, tuning forks—
robins and grosbeaks do a last soft shoe
in backyard Mountain Ash leaves.

Vibrations of impending migration
with a waxing moon rising over the Thunderchild Crabapple

lift my children's verve to a higher pitch
son and daughter swoon round the herb bed
under the rowan, rite of cut, dip, draw
hop-point: inarticulate praises, word-song singing.

Then brass and horn cease with their echoes
in our bones, the gathered moment at the end of a dance
running deep like the river, geese, receding motion.

Pheasant darkness pulls hearthward
bedtime for *sub specie aeternitatis.*

Feathered arms lift
feet trace   moon shadows.
Umbra of bird's breath.
To me! I say, *We'll follow the star's towpath.*
Mind those backyard ladybugs, now
burrowing under the leaves. Sh.
Our arms tilt through the trees
form our family vee.

When snow fogs ponds
my children scry for reflections
of the universe, find Granny and Granddad
and all the old stories Papa told
homing

in the way they form their sentences
as the steam of the morning pools in drops
of pancake batter, syrup—
In the girl's hand, a spatula.

World of snow outside, steam inside
and a boy emerges from the milky warmth
of his rumpled blankets, the wings
of his bed hair
smoothed by river current. The sand
he rubs from his eyes, stardust.
He espies his sister
kneeling on a chair at the kitchen counter
over her breakfast art.
Their eyes meet and in them
a congregating caesurae

and we hear the horn of the navigators
pass over the house.

Three Crosses

Throaty summer women pause
knee-deep in field cool grasses.
One looks back along the lure of city neon
night's heat breast high
lifts sighs of pleasure into the indigo night.

She draws herself up the grassy slope
joins the other two, their laughter
stilled as night's dark mirror springs forth.
The crow's head plunged under its wing
speaks words of reconciliation.

These three on the hill's knee
friends flocking
through the summer's discourse
not as prepared as they profess
to take on tethers of freedom or other ideals

and why would they? Three crosses on the hillside
emblazoned with the centuries' spiritual truth

there can be no map to guide their days
only the self, aging
who each meets along the way
and worship
and one another.

Faith, flight,
or coming home.

Homemaking

*what I want and all my days I pine for is to go back to my house
and see my day of homecoming*
– Homer, *The Odyssey*

As I push the vacuum back and forth
the children scream from room to room
leap over the mechanical beast
dive on the safe ground of a bed.

I let the playdream build a blueprint
based on the architecture of my past—
my mother, with the house in perfect order.

These days without her
I round a corner
find a mirror and see

a child streak across my path, followed
by another, they create
the place they will want to get back to.

Images neatly labelled, dated and stacked.
My mother hoeing potato hills
in late morning heat. I walk up the road from the river
across the bridge, over the railroad tracks, and up the gravel rise
sure of my welcome, the dogs running up the path.

The universe whispers aha
vista expands in heat, the hoe, my boots, her soft smile.

My children, each with a cleaning-rag
sing with cloths whirling over toy surfaces,
furniture legs, and up the stairs, along the banister.

Dishes washed, carpets upright, cookies baked and decorated
we build houses out of playdough
each linked with ways of halls and stairs
with little chairs and children
arms upraised, "Carry me,"
at the end of the day.

Yamnuska

The mountain basks in a strobe-lit memory of a long ago afternoon

        or does it

not wait at the edge of the foothills,
flat brow
its forehead like a skull inside of which are footprints
into the alpine larch and grey owls

the aftermath of another sunrise

        it does

as if yesterday's girls were meant to achieve all the zeniths
of their primed bodies
and stutter into their intellects
sans moon, sans night

with only the glow of another sunrise,
footprints, dewdrops, owl pellets
to guide them, maidens and aunts
mothers and daughters, to ritual
with ochre paints and bison skulls.
The days grow old without us.

Nightingales and Time
for Leslie

A thing of beauty is a joy forever
– John Keats, "Endymion"

Against her I am a fluttering thing
stilled and admired
held briefly on her outstretched hand
as she sits on a moss-etched stone bench.

She is a nymph naïve and naked
who strolls to the wellspring
follows the dip and skim of my thoughts
through shadows and sun on the path.

Like a seed blown in from heaven
I perch on the lip of the world
lure her into the liquid
a water lily tugged by current and flow.

She believes, briefly, the old stories
of nightingales and time, the eleven swans of the lake,
the order of the world where I am a songthing
and she is the goddess who swims in the lake.

Ovulation Symphony

Last year's sunflower husks
woke me before dawn.
Their faded centres rustling on cello poles
lured me to ritual
with ovum
in spring snow.

Under the Earth
sweet voices in rain cantos
herald the curlicue
fur of the egg
winding out
through its dark bed.

Near me, snow melt from the eavestrough
plummets to Earth
snaps silent the corner bed's tambourines.

Did I say blindly? The ovum
has its own way of seeing things
through stigma into the forest sea

and it is winter, a merlin falcon swims through the sky
its chitters echo in the womb's muscular dome.

Over the Moon

Spoon, a lover's posture
I am ladled into your mind

like curvy macaroni
in blue spirit smoke
above broth canoodled in a cup.

Aroma trigger
for memories glimpsed
in the oven's glass
in the flour's tracings
across the face.

How we got here:

A blessing
      a ring of joined hands
      round the dinner table
chatter and clattersounds.
The household hound noses in
when dishes are pushed past the elbows
wags his whole body in ceremonial farewell
when guests find their coats and depart
voices on the crisp wind.

We find
  a place to curl up in
  when, addled by love
  fed to the brim
  sleep takes us in.

A Sentinel Among the Herds

All day checking the fences
hammer in hand
waves of grass moving across hills.

Up at the house
there is a centaur outside the bedroom window
arms folded against the wind.

I sleep in my room
am wakened alive in the dark
the burning woman standing
in a lighted mansion.

And all night under starlight
the herds move in and out of paddocks and fields.

I follow the light through the forest
though the way is not easy.

The evening rose changes with the mourning
doves arriving, and geese in a field.

This morning, the colours
are pastel
white on green
browns
stripes layers needles
and knitting
pine cones strung together
growing on a tree
a sweater
covering me.

Walk up from the valley
remembering (to close the gate)

within the breathing winds of the forest
the flowers bloom unseen.

Fruits and Offerings

A golden retriever stretches out in the kitchen.
Thumps his tail when I climb
over-and-back, counter-to-fridge,
over-and-back, table-to-sink.

Down the hall my son emerges from his bedroom,
pushes Laddie gently back to the floor,
uses the big dog for a pillow.
Their settling on linoleum an act of ritual.

I chop carrots, onions, peppers
haul pans of water, season beef broth.

My son's running commentary heartsease and fennel.
Basil-bright, my daughter greens past
finds her seat at my grandmother's table
kneels on her chair, interjects red petals, laughs, "Mama!"
as I arrange paper, brushes, paints before her.

Windows fog around the warm aromatic alcove.

My son with Laddie's front leg
over the crook of his neck: "Look!
he's got me—I can't get up!"

The front door lock keys open.
Laddie rises, my son springs to his feet.
My daughter's laughter, "Daddy,
I made a painting—a flower—see!"

Under his arm, a loaf of French bread
a bottle of wine. In the altar of this tiny space
fruits and offerings, rainbow from his eyes to mine.

Non-human Voices

An uncertain moon last night
and the goat wind scouring through mountain chutes
rattling the window panes, while the fir
framed right into the lodge's balcony
dresses in white gloss, and sways, her fingers
trailing across the balcony's glass.

A snow clump, airily soft lifts from the fir
on an updraft, its fine white individuality
swirls up, commingling with chimney soot.

The tree's fronds are filigree, her green nettles jingle.
The wind thinks he can orchestrate everything. But
even he has to stop to take a breath
between songs. The fir stirs and bends.
Her breath hole is a slit above the balcony's floor.

Standing beside her cold dark limbs
or inside with the porch glass snugged shut

I language her messages
brew tea and write them down.

Black and White

The performance yielded its silver angel shine
in lights, in perfumed words;
its yellow and red angels, those of anger and jealousy
guarded by audience members and children
those who shielded their lights in darkness
belittled by the infelicities of their attention
now gilded and hung upon the silvery tongues
now darting into recesses of personal imagination.

Poetry performances do this. And when
the recorders fluted their medieval songs
tapestries of woven angels danced psyche
danced storm. Brought the clash of symbols
to the kissed lips of silence
and applause.

Strongroom

I have a key
a memory

and Alberta soil in my bones.
One iota of Minas Basin red clay
a revenant at the gate.

"It's not locked," I say.

She would have held me dear
in the dyke-lee
looking out to Blomidon, long ago.
She in red, me in blue
our windbreakers birdheads
on the edge of the tidal flats
below the soccer fields
in Sunday weather.

But that was shared history, Mary
before we saw your sister act in *Brigadoon*
and our laughter shimmed the last VIA rail car
with our foreign accents, and our arms out to the rail
holding on for dear life with throats raised to heaven
swaying on the platform between two cars
"Farewell to Nova Scotia," top of the lungs.

I called her, twice, from that other shore
with in-laws listening in
and the cedars, dark in the back yard.
"What did you say your name was?"
she asked. And the wind took our windbreakers
lifted them like flags over Acadia
remnants shouted into the past.

Christmas Baggage

Come home, come home now with me —
I'll open all the windows, give my winter coat away.

Don't listen to those shadows at the river's edge,
the songs they sing inside the scatterings of wind.

Small song for the balsam poplar
           Jan Zwicky

Seven sweet days from the alarm clock's angry face,
and the wedge of cars in parking lots
(no wonder the power steering failed
—our arms so often in that circumambient groove
as if the gesture had more meaning than getting in
and out of a mountain of errands tricky as scree.)
Even the smell of our city, its affluence
mixed with the old bag smell of cart-pushing people
a skin-scent wind-washed with my plea
come home, come home now with me —

It is a small thing to wish for an anchor.
I am adrift again on the wolf willow route
with balsam poplar's woody chuckle
and raven's wings a wink to the season's mind-bash.
In the river valley with snow all round, quiet sun above
and wrestling with the question of why giving can be so complicated.
Christ in manger scenes, the Bible's message of beginnings,
Isaiah's prophecies about the Messiah giving his life away.
Let our need for permanence go then, but use restraint, okay?
I'll open all the windows, give my winter coat away.

Do you see how hard this is, to escape the folded suitcase
to lug only the essentials, leave our ancestors to their rest?
How the past informs even as its snake-charm sloughs its form?
Ha! Eleven or fifteen of us around the table with patriarchs
informing the tenor of tales told, being deferential with one another.
It's Christmas dinner festooned with stars, gold, silver, sage-scent.
Candles, humour, straight-shooting—it's all a practice
at least what led up to this is, a mirror room
pristine as meditation, free speech, the ghost's nudge.
Don't listen to those shadows at the river's edge,

translating what they know, for this crowd
would be a triumph, like longevity, bloodlines, kinship
and we each control an hourglass, for measuring the length
of those shadows at holiday's end, the calm aftershock of goodbye
played out in doorways, parking lots, the touch
of a loved-one's rescinded manipulative gesture, a gift:
It's Christmas, a time for homing in on innocence,
the babe's voice in the wilderness, willow's rush, spirit's fruit.
I'll heed their tang's pulp beneath the rind
the songs they sing inside the scatterings of wind.

Ivory Willow

Daydrift thickens
like bracken
woven into useful willow chairs.

Sit on the deck
watch the world go by.

Heave myself upright
sweat glues my dress
to thigh backs and buttocks.
A butterfly lands on my breasts.

A butterfly lands on my breasts
while editing mother poems
the summer melding
into a single day.

I think it was Sidney who said poetry
is "the dreams of them that are awake."
Let it be night again
when the inky black closes in
murmuring just-heard conversations
along the shorelines like a calligraphy pen
drawing curtains and a deep, wide bed.

Metaphorica

On Sundays, we speak long-distance
phone conversations search the caverns of the soul
stalagmites
stalactites

and even in our natural form
there is no need for the fig leaf, sister
(though I'd wear a peacock feather fan
to hide my waist, paint roses on my nipples
and cup exquisite cerulean tattoos
emanating from my cleavage
a twined Uroborus
round my breasts).

The scorching memories we sweep together
into full-sized rundlestone hearths, a chore.

Plotinus notes soul's circularity
its motion patterns on a seashell
whorls on a fingertip, and true to its nature
it works, striving when it will
enacting ritual
sorting remembrance in its amphitheatre
with pantheons of stone-eyed metanoia
offering insight to the way we are.

Sometimes visions, this circling
drifts out and in, expanding and contracting
like a pulsar
a breath of reason upon imagination.

But we tarry at our chore, sister.
These embers will fade, today, I think
and we must to the surface again. To the
upper chambers where we will say our goodbyes
though the mirror in your eyes
says "Father" and mine, "Mother"
we do have our separate ways.

And I, for one, laugh at the shocking
actions of my daytime self as much
as at what the dream reveals.

It's an advantage to have this point of view
sisterly vantage, the crow's cawing
keeps me awake.

Hillman asks, *Is the soul made with guilt?*
You know the answer, sister, though Guilt
wears a crown in the soul's chamber
waves her wand around. Sparks fly.
We banish her so the guardians of sleep
may tuck the crow's head under its wing.

I can neither understand nor manage
these personages who I've built in my soul.
The nursery-rhyme mothers, their scampering offspring
Hades, gods of war, statues, angels, fawns and nymphs.
O wonderful denizens of these halls
the Cook's triumph and constant prepping
serves up the feast when it's called for
while the mythic creatures come and go.

While the mythic creatures come and go
I search for the appropriate altar
because I want to bend my knee
curtsy, even, and all they ask for
or will receive, is my love.

Curiosity Cabinet

I cup a perfect moonshell
to my ear and stand before the cabinet
in black-eyed contemplation
of bone flutes, birch bark, dried moss
last year's rosebud arranged
in a clear-topped box.

No sound but the sea, sighing
and here, here in Alberta,
so far from the sea
I replace the shell, catch my quizzical
look in the glass front door of the cabinet
and migrate, with the daylight, out the back door,
leather leash in hand.

Just Alberta skies over birch
with a freezing river nearby
the dog, the underbrush
and a raven high up in a nest.

Her black-eyed observation
over dipthong
wind-carried, obvious, and I believe
she would if she could
put one foot after another
while the dog carries a stick.
After all, I would if I could
perch black-ruffled and imperious
up high in the birch.

My dance in harmony
with the Saskatchewan's ice breaking.
All my melodies carried
until like carrion I become part of a raven
with a raven's past and purpose
of riding wind waves
passing all the stimuli to eyes
to search the wind for spaces
in which to dance.

Months later, my footsteps
crunch leaves under the high winds
the twilit sky. There is no-one in the high nest,
its mass of branches wooden, grey.
Day has ended and there is no moon.

Back home I think to latch the gate
boil the kettle for tea. I shrug off
my light sweater. A yellow
crinkly leaf fragments under my fingertips
when I brush the hair from my eyes.

In the night forest there are no footsteps.
At home there is no knock at my gate.

Bead-bright eyes, fingering treasures
in the curiosity cabinet
my laughter a glottal stop, dipthong croak

curiouser and curiouser, I light the lamp
see wave after wave of reflection
my black feathered face.

I fly, once around the room
then settle on an upholstered perch.

Advice from Western Canadian Rockies

Hide grows winter coat, tufts in ears
sounds muffled in snow, the world white
in spots, granite, mossy, crags, the caves

where bears are sleeping their round bellies
easing up on breath, down on breath
this gentle rhythm

you see partridge and piano wire as traps
avoid putting your paw down
where it'll get shot off, or worse

and you tell of hunting only what you need
caching plenty, being wary
not so much wrong with that, cougar cat.

Schooling

Allow me my references to this ancient school
for it is where I had my beginnings

gate and willow fen

determining my cosmic place
in this part of the world: horse and hay

hallowed stable and starry night
chill air and equal parts:　　　snow and ice
hay and oats

contriving to feed the champion feed
acting on the learned lore of horsemen
exacting calculus: a handful of stars　　a jar
of wishes

long childhood hair a-straggle about my face
learning the basics of grooming:
the possibilities and necessities of　　curry brush
hoof pick
dandy brush

and for myself: mirror of discord.

Be quick, agile, with the eagle of theory above you
the ancient owls of history behind you
test stamina of spirit

race with strength and energy, become one at once
with the ancient method of training
a juxtaposition of victory over honor
animal vs. woman

heart

Horse at Work

Horse crossed her legs
and tried to look prim.

Those bits of straw in her hair
behind her ear detracted from the picture.

Horse rose sturdily from the boardroom table
trotted down the hall, disappeared around a corner.

Only the scent of her and the rhythmic clip clop
of her black boots. She settled in the bathroom

caught between stall walls
and the mirrors, she worked fingers through her mane

smiled a toothy smile at herself and left.
The rest of the herd milling in the hallway shifted

made room for her purses and briefcase
red and black leather. Her coat so warm.

As they stand there part of the elevator queue
doors open, flocks of sparrows quoting Xenophon.

One buzzes her cheek with a wing tip, another pecks
at the seeds in steaming manure by her boots.

Someone lifts a halter from behind her back
Horse nuzzles for carrots and walks placidly into the shaft.

Horse under Saddle

She's back in her office
silent as stone

only the sparrows
nesting and the tractor

outside the window.
Horse prods the end of a pencil

with big teeth. Blows
air through her lips

turns on her laptop
adjusts the girth

smooths the saddle flaps.
She arches her neck round

to watch as her rider
straddles her, hands on reins.

She apt to take the bit
in her mouth and run

but a glance at the daytimer
and she cocks her ears

listening for direction
and moving with measured grace

down the length of the arena
and across the page

asking herself as fingers
flit across the keys

am I the horse
or the rider?

her new Prestige saddle
black Italian leather

and the Lamy calligraphy pen
tools of the trade.

Heart of Oak

Singed hoof smoke spread
its dragon breath from the farrier's forge
his red truck backed up to the rain-pelt
under the eave with lick-your-lips rain
drumming down. Saddle horses in the paddocks
with their black coats runneling.

Dank in the dark depths of the shed row
horses waiting the farrier's tools
peal cries and are answered from the distant green

where, dandelion heads tucked in their lips in the rain
succulent fescue dribbling down,
they answer, and my gelding stomps
crowds me on this quick-cloud day, the sun sudden
through the stall window, flicks his tail.

I take him for obedience class, just
me and him in the moist dirt arena.
Muriel watches from the end-seats
and Linda comes in to sweep the boards.

Iser postures his challenge
his eye upon me with this discourse
as if winged, his hooves, as if winged

the lunge line of our spell shrinks the world
to a 20-metre-diameter circle
to voice and trust
whip and forward into tee-rot, and can-ter.

He wants to show me what he knows
more than what he can do: win a
marathon stakes race, the Heart of Oak,
wire-to-wire. He can race, but his pride
comes in showing how easy it is to learn
as long as I command respect
and let him go.

A Woman is Strong

I am a mountain in morning sunlight
my facets move in pink organza
lilac blush
                upon my crags wild goats
                feed on sorrel, white flowers

stretch their lithe bodies across cracks.
The abyss means nothing to their wilful ways.

Who can say the nymph of the brook
is a desperado—look

she has surrounded herself with modest ferns
and above her canopy, the pipes, the pipes!

Suite #6

I bring you laughter
caught in the most delicate seaweed
on the beach at low tide
its purple filaments yielding salty
brouhahas from the depths.

I bring you love scraped from the roof
of a cave where firelight flickered
and fragrant smoke licked the walls
while campfire talk spilled onto embers.

I bring you fierce belief in yourself
that you may go out from this cave
and find seashell lyrics and sand-dollar lullabies.
Keep them sweet in your still, deep evermore.

Notes and Acknowledgements

Thank you to the Writer's Guild of Alberta for arranging fantastic writing retreats with beautiful environs and stimulating company at The Banff Centre and Strawberry Creek. Thanks also to the colleagues and friends who encouraged me over the many years of this book's making: Leslie McBride, Shawna Lemay, Kath Maclean, Kathy Fisher, Sandra Mooney-Ellerbeck, and Anne Gerard Marshall. For their wit and wisdom, their tidings and omens, I thank the Magpies—Julie Robinson, Rusti Lehay, Myrna Garanis and Anna Mioduchowska. I thank the Stroll of Poets Society, which has hosted Poet's Haven for years, providing fellowship, community and readings. Special thanks to Theresa Agnew for proofreading the page proofs.

I thank St. John the Evangelist parish and in particular Mary-Ann Provencal for offering perspective and direction.

I am grateful to Ellen Drews-Ortlieb and the horses at Amberlea Meadows, particularly Riley Joe—you've taught me a lot about spirit, trust, and the benefits of having a "poised mind." Richard Olafson, the poet behind Ekstasis Editions, thank you for making me a part of your unique publishing program.

Loving thanks to Phil, Andrew, Sarah and Laddie; and to my extended families for the stories, holidays together, and laughter.

Epigraph. John Gregory. *The Neoplatonists*. London: Kyle Cathie. 1991. p. 184.

Ancestors and Angels. The epigraph is from Shakespeare's *Antony and Cleopatra*.

"Birth." *Theosis* expresses the idea that the Holy Spirit intends that our lives should be deified, holy, and echoes the notion of living "in Christ."

"Shipshape." The epigraph is from George Mackay Brown. *Greenvoe*,

London: Hogarth Press, 1972. pp.76-77.

"An Early Grace." My Dad's friends were Catholics—Catlickers, and Protestants—Potlickers—names they'd taunt at one another once, on their way to school as a gang, they'd part ways to their separate schools.

"Spiritual Canticle." William McNamara O.C.D. writes about faith allowing us to see our lives against a "background of eternity" using a perspective that is focused on the divine. (In *The Art of Being Human* (1967).) "Spiritual Canticle" is also the title of a work by St. John of the Cross that expresses the idea that God, who we crave, is within each of us.

Fieldgrass Conversations. The lines by W.S. Merwin come from *Migration*, Washington: Copper Canyon Press, 2005.

"Church Bells" was originally published in *Eyeing the Magpie*, Edmonton: Five Magpie Press, 2008.

"Fruiting." The Henning Mankell quote comes from *Before the Frost*, New York: New Press. Distributed by W.W. Norton, 2005, [c2004]. p. 32.

"Ave Verum Corpus" means *hail, true body*, and refers here to a short Eucharistic hymn. This poem was originally published under the title "On Moraine Hill" in *Running Barefoot: Women Write the Land*, Edmonton: Rowan Books, 2001.

"Collaboration" was originally published in *Eyeing the Magpie*.

"Field Glasses" was published in *Lake: A Journal of Art and the Environment*, 2010. *Corpus pontiflex*: The written word building a bridge between God and humans.

"Truce" was published in *The Stroll of Poets Killer Blinks Anthology*, Edmonton: Stroll of Poets Society, 2008.

Gate and Willow Fen. The epigraph comes from "Grace" in Kevin Crossley-Holland, *Poems from East Anglia*, London: Enitharmon; Chester Springs, PA: Dufour Editions, 1997.

"Longing for the Greatest Thing." The epigraph (and the title of the poem) is by Gregory of Nazianzus, as quoted in Thomas C. Oden and Joel C. Elowsky, *We Believe in the Holy Spirit*, USA: The Institute of Classical Studies, 2009, page 73. The last two lines are from *The Summa Theologica*, Saint Thomas Aquinas. Translated by fathers of the English Dominican Province, Rev. by Daniel J. Sullivan, Volume 2, Chicago: Enclyclopaedia Britannica, 1952, page 378.

"Strawberry Creek" was published in *Carte Blanche*, Issue 10, Quebec Writer's Federation, Online Journal, 2009.

"The River." The epigraph is from James Hillman, *A Blue Fire*, New York: HarperCollins Publishers, p.75.

"Rain, Wiwaxy Peaks, Lake O'Hara." The poem's title comes from the title of a painting by J.E.H. Macdonald. The epigraph is from J.E.H. Macdonald. *Journal Entry*: Thursday, 10 September 1925. Samuel Allen of the Lake Louise Club penned the lines about the *wind in the tamarack boughs* in his Alpine Journal of 1896, as noted in *Mountaineering in the Canadian Rockies*. The *emerald and violet...* italicized words are from J.E.H. MacDonald, *The Canadian Bookman*, (vol.) vi, (no.) 11 (November 1924) page 229.

"Pining" was published in *The Society*, St. Peter's College, Saskatchewan, 2009.

"Autumn Crescendo." *sub specie aeternitatis:* is an attempt to see the world from the point of view of eternity, and children, with so little past to bring into their present, are very much future oriented, yet their circumstance is one of having been newly birthed from eternity.

"Umbilical." In *Tractates on the Gospel of John* Augustine writes that the Spirit of God moans in us like a dove. 6.2. He moans in us because we are separate from God. Doves moan in love and the Spirit chose to be represented as a dove through which he might moan. And the Spirit moans in us that we might be united with the Father and the Son.

"Three Crosses." Part of *Cortex 2007*, a performance of poetry, dance and visual art. Written in response to Nicole Pakan's photograph of the same name.

"Christmas Baggage." Jan Zwicky. "Small song for the balsam poplar" in *Thirty-seven Small Songs & Thirteen Silences*, Kentville, Nova Scotia: Gaspereau Press, 2005.

"Metaphorica." The italicized quote refers to James Hillman and his book *The Myth of Analysis*. Illinois: Northwestern University Press. 1997. p. 197. Hillman also refers to metaphorica in his book as a way of describing how archetypes are wondrous and therefore memorable, and by cultivating memory, we build soul. For references to Plotinus' view, please see the epigraph to *Communion*.

"A Woman is Strong." First published in *Eyeing the Magpie*.